GALE SAYERS
STAR RUNNING BACK

GALE SAYERS
STAR RUNNING BACK

by Julian May

Published by Crestwood House, Inc., Mankato, Minnesota 56001. Published simultaneously in Canada by J. M. Dent and Sons, Ltd. Library of Congress Catalog Card Number: 73-80424. International Standard Book Number: 0-913940-04-6. Text copyright © 1973 by Julian May Dikty. Illustrations copyright © 1973 by Crestwood House, Inc. All rights reserved. No part of this book may be reproduced in any form without written permission from the publisher, except for brief passages included in a review. Printed in the United States of America.

Designed by William Dichtl

Crestwood House, Inc., Mankato, Minn. 56001

PHOTOGRAPHIC CREDITS

GALE SAYERS
STAR RUNNING BACK

The pro football star was talking to the kids at an inner city school.

He said: "I'll bet some of you would just as soon forget about books and classes."

The boys laughed. "All *riiiight*!" one yelled.

The football star said: "An older man I know could have been a lawyer. His uncle offered to send him to college. But he dropped out of high school instead. He wanted to get a job, make some money, and maybe buy a car."

"Yeah!" said a kid.

The football player went on. "So this man got his job. And after 33 years, he's still working. But instead of being a lawyer and wearing nice clothes and working nice hours, this man works as a car polisher in a used-car lot."

One boy snickered. But most of the rest were quiet.

"That man was my father," said Gale Sayers.

His parents were expecting a girl baby when he was born. So they gave him a girl's name. But the word *gale* also means "a strong wind." So maybe it wasn't such a bad name for a boy who would grow up to be one of football's greatest running backs.

Gale Sayers was born in Wichita, Kansas in 1943. When he was eight, the family moved to the large city of Omaha, Nebraska.

They were very poor. Sometimes Gale and his older brother, Win, shot sparrows with a BB gun. Mrs. Sayers cooked the birds for dinner. They had nothing else.

Gale Sayers and his parents, Bernice Ross Sayers and Roger Winfield Sayers, Sr. The photograph was taken in 1965 when Gale received an award proclaiming him "Omaha's Greatest Pro Football Player."

The Howard Kennedy School football team, 1957. Gale Sayers is at far right, second row. Win Sayers is second from the right, first row.

Win Sayers was a good student, but Gale was only interested in sports. The boys were one grade apart at Howard Kennedy School. There a strong coach named Robert Rose taught the boys football, basketball, and track. Gale and Win liked football best. They were both fullbacks.

The Kennedy midget-league football team won the state championship in 1957. Win Sayers, in eighth grade, was the star.

"I'm going to score more than you next year," Gale told his brother.

And he did, too. Kennedy won the championship again in 1958 and this time Gale was top scorer.

Gale Sayers *(far right)* starts downfield for a score in a game played by Omaha Central High School.

Coach Frank Smagacz of Omaha Central High School

Win Sayers went on to Central High, a college prep school. So Gale had to go there, too, even though his grades weren't very good. There was no way Gale could beat his brother in studies. But sports were something else.

In his freshman year, Gale helped the frosh football team to its first intercity championship in 23 years. He was the speediest boy that Coach Frank Smagacz had ever seen. Nobody could catch him.

The coach couldn't believe his good luck. Win Sayers was an outstanding football player and a track star as well. But it looked like his little brother, Gale, would be even better!

That summer, Gale grew three inches and gained 50 pounds. When he tried sprinting in the fall, his old speed was gone.

"What's wrong, Gale?" Coach Smagacz asked.

"I grew too much, too fast," Gale said sadly. "My speed just didn't keep up with me. Maybe all this new growth will help me in football, though."

He became a linebacker, then switched to second-string offense. But it wasn't until late in the season that he felt his body was again doing what he wanted it to do.

Meanwhile, Win Sayers won the intercity scoring championship in football and was a sprinting champ, too.

Gale became an outstanding broad-jumper in high school.

Gale felt that he just had to do better than his brother. He was always practicing. He felt that if he worked hard enough, he could do whatever he wanted.

When Gale was a Junior, his older brother pulled a muscle and was put out of action. Immediately, Gale stepped into his shoes as the team's star running back. Gale was intercity football scoring champion that year and the next. His wonderful speed had returned.

He also won medals in hurdling and jumping. One of his broad jumps—24 feet 11¾ inches—was a state high-school record that stood for many years.

The Sayers brothers *(left to right):* Roger Winfield, Jr. (Win), Ronnie, Gale.

In class, Gale Sayers was a goof-off and a rebel. He had a good brain, but he was shy and unable to express himself in speaking or writing.

On the athletic field, he became a different person. Out there, he didn't have to talk, didn't have to rack his brain to gain a victory.

It all came naturally. And using the talent he was born with, he became Omaha's top high-school athlete.

Gale played in the Shrine All-Star game in the summer of 1961.

Gale *(left)* and his best friend Vernon Breakfield were both outstanding high-school athletes. Vern went along with Gale as he visited 17 different colleges, trying to decide which one to attend.

Most high-school football stars want to go on to college. But Gale didn't give it a thought until he met a girl named Linda McNeil.

She was a good student, the youngest of five children. Her family couldn't help thinking of her as "the baby." But Linda didn't want to have people take care of her. She was a strong person who wanted to help others.

She knew, somehow, that big, strong Gale Sayers needed her. She pushed him until he agreed to go to college. She helped him bring his grades up, too.

In Gale's senior year, more than a hundred colleges offered him football scholarships. He finally chose the University of Kansas.

And he and Linda agreed that they would get married after he completed his freshman year.

14

Gale carries the ball in a game against Texas Christian University.

The first year at college was very hard for Gale. He was a shy boy from the black slums of Omaha, a boy who had not yet learned how to study.

The one thing he could do well was play football. The freshman team spent most of its time scrimmaging with the varsity. But they did get a chance to play two games, and Gale starred in both of them.

In the first game, they beat Kansas State's frosh squad, 21-6. Gale scored all three touchdowns. The second game, against the Missouri freshmen, was tied 21-21. Once again, Gale made all the scoring runs. And they started calling him "Gale the Jet."

In 1962, Coach Jack Mitchell promoted Gale to the varsity. He became number-two rusher in the Big Eight Conference.

16

He and Linda were married the next summer. With her help, he finally learned how to study and began to get good grades.

Coach Jack Mitchell promoted Gale to the varsity that fall. In the first game, against Texas Christian, Gale carried the ball 27 times for 114 yards. But Kansas lost, 6-3.

In the three games that followed, Gale continued to carry the ball. He was a master at faking and changing his pace. When tacklers dived for him, Gale was somewhere else. The team began to win.

Gale and Linda Sayers in their student apartment.

In a game against the University of Oklahoma in 1963, Gale starts a 61-yard touchdown run behind quarterback Steve Renko.

Gale injured his hand in the fifth game and told the coach he wanted to sit the next one out. But Coach Mitchell said:

"I know your hand hurts. But if we tape it, it'll be all right. If you were really injured, I'd take you out. But there's a difference between injury and pain. Everybody plays football with pain."

Gale played. He carried the ball 22 times in that game against Oklahoma State, gaining 283 yards. It was a Big Eight record. One of his touchdown runs was 96 yards from scrimmage.

When they won, 36-17, Gale forgot the pain.

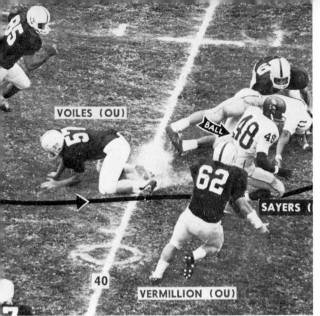
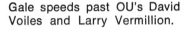

Gale speeds past OU's David Voiles and Larry Vermillion.

He appears to be cornered at the 45-yard line!

In Gale's junior year, the Kansas team played their arch-rival, the University of Nebraska. Kansas went scoreless until the third quarter, when they managed a field goal. With the score 10-3 in the fourth quarter, Nebraska ran out of steam and had to punt. The ball went out of bounds on the Kansas one-foot line.

The Nebraska defense loomed like a concrete wall. So the Kansas quarterback took a long chance and pitched the ball to Gale at right halfback. He started around left end. A teammate gave him a good block and he slithered past two other Nebraska tacklers. Then it was clear sailing for a touchdown run, the longest of his college career: 99 yards.

But Gale dodges to the right past Sooner halfback Larry Shields.

Gale made All-American as both a junior and senior. He broke most of the Big Eight conference rushing records. His three-year total rushing yardage was 2,675. Still, when Kansas chose its Most Valuable Player after the 1964 season, the honor went to a white defense man instead of to Gale.

He catches Charley Mayhue off balance and streaks for a touchdown.

That hurt him deeply. He became more active in matters of race relations. In spring, there was a demonstration to protest segregated housing. Black and white students staged a sit-in. When the peaceful demonstrators were arrested, Gale went to jail, too.

Brian Piccolo, who graduated from Wake Forest College, was Most Valuable Player of the Atlantic Coast Conference. In 1964 he earned the national rushing title with 1,044 yards and the national scoring title with 111 points.

Coach George Halas gives some advice to rookie Gale Sayers.

The pro football scouts had been watching Gale for a long time. Some said he was as good as Jim Brown, Cleveland's great running back. Others compared Gale to Lenny Moore of the Baltimore Colts.

Many teams tried to get Gale. He finally signed with the Chicago Bears. In June 1965 he played in the Coach's All-America game and met two other Bear rookies. Dick Butkus was a star linebacker from the University of Illinois. Brian Piccolo was a Wake Forest back.

When Gale first met Brian, all he said was, "Hello." Later, Piccolo was injured in practice and couldn't play. Gale thought: *Too bad,* and then forgot about it. He himself had never been seriously hurt playing football.

When the two rookie backs reported to camp, owner-coach George Halas put Gale Sayers on the active list. Brian Piccolo, still limping, only made the taxi squad.

The Chicago Bears were in trouble in 1965. Two years before, they had been NFL champions. But the next year, injuries took their toll and the team nose-dived to sixth. They had quarterback trouble and the ground offense was very weak.

Gruff old George Halas had pulled his Bears out of worse spots before. Now he was counting heavily on Gale Sayers, bringing him along slowly in the first two exhibition games, not letting him do much.

George Halas, the "Papa Bear," is one of football's all-time greats. In the 1920's, he was a star end, later elected to the Hall of Fame. He helped found the American Professional Football Association in 1919; it later became the NFL. He also helped found the Chicago Bears in 1922, leading the team to greatness in the 30's. After World War II service in the Navy, Halas took up coaching again, finally retiring in 1955. But he could not stay on the sidelines. In 1958 he came back as head coach. In 1965, when Gale Sayers joined the team, Halas was 70 years old.

In the third exhibition game, against the Rams, Halas turned Gale loose.

The Rams punted and Gale ran the ball 77 yards. It was his first pro touchdown.

Then he went 93 yards in a kickoff return. Halas watched, glum-looking on the outside, happy inside. Still later, Gale used the halfback-option play. Trapped by the Rams defense, he passed to a teammate who went romping over the goal-line. The Bears won, 28-14.

Gale Sayers *(40)* makes a three-yard gain against the Packers. Mike Ditka *(89)* blocks.

The regular season began. Halas started with Jon Arnett as halfback. Gale only carried the ball once in the game and the team lost to the 49ers, 55-24. The second game was lost to the Rams. But Gale scored a touchdown in his lone play.

At last George Halas allowed Gale to start, even though he knew the rookie was still learning. They played Green Bay and lost, 23-14. Gale scored both touchdowns. He also nailed down a job as starting halfback.

Gale relaxes at home with some of his trophies and mementos.

They played their first home game of the season against the Rams. The Chicago fans were on the lookout for number 40, rookie Gale Sayers. And he showed them what he could do.

Taking a screen pass on the Bears' 20-yard line, he ran 80 yards for a touchdown in spite of being smashed by the giant Ram tackle, Rosey Grier.

Later, he helped the team to score again by firing an option pass 26 yards to Dick Gordon. The Bears won, 31-6.

28

The next Sunday they faced the Minnesota Vikings. It was an exciting, seesaw game. The Bears were ahead, 17-13, at half-time. In the last seconds of the third quarter, Gale scored a touchdown after shaking off two defenders. In the fourth period, he scored again.

But then the Vikings rallied. With only two minutes to go in the game, Minnesota led 37-31. Coach Norm Van Brocklin told his kicker to keep the ball away from Gale Sayers—no matter how. But Gale grabbed the kickoff anyway and ran it 96 yards for a touchdown.

In the first quarter of the Bears-Vikings game, Gale picks up 8 yards and a first down. Vikings George Rose *(44)* and Jim Marshall *(70)* bring Gale down.

In the fourth quarter of the game against the Vikings, Gale romps 96 yards for a touchdown. Chasing him in vain are Dave Osborn *(41)*, Tom Hall *(28)*, and Jim Marshall *(70)*.

He topped that performance almost at once. Dick Butkus intercepted a Viking pass and took it to Minnesota's 11-yard line. Gale crashed through the waiting Vikings and scored again.

A television sportscaster ran up after the play. "This really must have been something for you, Gale! Was this the highlight of your career?"

Still nervous and shy, Gale said, "Nope," and rushed away. Some people thought he was being rude. But he really had not yet learned how to handle fame.

Gale dodges Kermit Alexander of the San Francisco 49ers.

Fame had its price. The message went out to enemy defensemen: "Get Sayers." The Bears won the next two games, against the Lions and the Packers. But Gale was held down when the opposition zeroed in on him.

The next week, Baltimore topped the Bears on a disputed call. Gale rushed only 17 yards in 11 attempts. But he was still learning. He was starting to acquire the pro football player's instinct that tells where the blockers will be—and how to avoid them.

Chicago won the next four, and Gale was in there working each time.

They met the San Francisco 49ers again on December 12. Chicago's Wrigley Field was a muddy mess. But on the Bears' first play, Bear quarterback Rudy Bukich called a screen pass. Gale took it on the Bears' 20, cut around a gang of 49ers, took advantage of a block, and kept cutting and wiggling through the line. A tiny opening showed and Gale put on steam. In a split second he was through and running. It was an 80-yard touchdown. The 46,000 Bear fans screamed approval.

Gale carries the ball 80 yards for a touchdown against San Francisco in the great game played December 12, 1965. The 49ers moving in are Elbert Kimbrough (45) and Jerry Martens (80).

In the second quarter of the San Francisco game, Gale shakes off Kermit Alexander *(39)* and runs 21 yards for another TD.

In the second quarter, he showed them some more. He scored twice, sweeping around left end. Early in the third quarter Bukich gave Gale a pitchout on the 50-yard line. He took off with it and scored.

Some people had called Gale a scatback—a runner with no real strength. Now he proved them wrong by crashing through the 49er line from the one-yard mark for his fifth touchdown of the day.

He had just tied Lenny Moore's record of 20 TD's in one season. The fans screamed! Could he beat it?

Is it a bird? A plane? No—it's Gale Sayers soaring through the 49er defense for a mud-splattered touchdown.

In the middle of the last period he grabbed a punt on the Bears' 15. It seemed like the whole San Francisco defense closed in on him. Cutting and swerving, out-running the whole pack of 49ers, he charged into the end zone. Then he threw the ball into the air and danced.

Six touchdowns in one game! It had been done only twice before in pro football—by Ernie Nevers in 1929 and by Dub Jones in 1951. If Gale went for seven, he would set an all-time record.

But the Bears had already won the game. Coach Halas did not want to risk Gale in another play. The crowd yelled: "We want Sayers!" But Jon Arnett made the last touchdown for a final score of 61-20.

This time, when someone asked Gale if the game had been his greatest football thrill, he said: "*One of the greatest.*"

The Bears played their last game against the Vikings. Gale scored touchdown number 22, a season record. He also led the league in scoring with 132 points.

He was a shoo-in for Rookie of the Year.

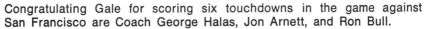

Congratulating Gale for scoring six touchdowns in the game against San Francisco are Coach George Halas, Jon Arnett, and Ron Bull.

The next season, Gale was as good as ever. But the team had quarterback trouble again and won only five games. George Halas said, "We can't win anything. So I want everybody to try to help Gale win the rushing title."

Gale's backup men that year were Jon Arnett and Brian Piccolo. But they could only take a little of the pressure off Gale, who had become a kind of one-man offense in a troubled team.

The last game of the 1966 season would decide whether Gale won the rushing title. He needed 97 yards to beat Leroy Kelly of the Cleveland Browns.

Gale's mother and father sat in the stands. It was the first time they had seen their son play pro football.

In the final game of the 1966 season, Gale outwits the Minnesota Vikings' defense. The Bears won, 41-28.

In a 1966 game against Baltimore, Gale eludes Colt defensive back Lenny Lyles and runs 10 yards for a touchdown. The Bears won, 27-17.

On the very first play, Gale returned the kickoff for a 90-yard touchdown. He scored again on a three-yard spurt. He helped set up two more touchdowns and two field goals. At the end of the game, he had rushed 197 yards and the title was his. His season total was 1,231 yards. He also set a league record for total yards gained in a season: 2,440.

At the Awards Dinner of the National Football League Players Association, the 1966 winners pose together. *From left to right:* Gale Sayers, Chicago Bears, rushing; Charley Taylor, Washington Redskins, pass receiving; Dave Lee, Baltimore Colts, punting; Johnny Roland, St. Louis Cardinals, offensive rookie of the year; Bruce Gossett, Los Angeles Rams, scoring.

Gale Sayers *(foreground, left)* heads into trouble in a 1967 game against Green Bay. Willie Davis *(87)* moves in for the tackle. Herb Adderley *(26)* and Dave Robinson *(89)* are also ready to stop Gale.

In 1967, Coach Halas decided he would integrate the team roommates on the road. They were paired by position. Gale roomed with his backup man, Brian Piccolo, and they became close friends.

The 1967 season was a disappointing one for Gale. He only finished third in rushing. The Bears came in fourth in the league.

When the season was over, Gale began to think about his future life, when he could no longer play ball. He went to school to learn how to become a stockbroker. The course was very hard, but Gale passed. He went to work for a Chicago brokerage firm in the off season.

Gale sits at his desk in a Chicago stock brokerage. The board records the rise and fall of stocks in the market.

As Kermit Alexander blocks Gale, the Chicago fullback's foot is still anchored in the grass. The picture shows the sickening moment of Gale's knee injury.

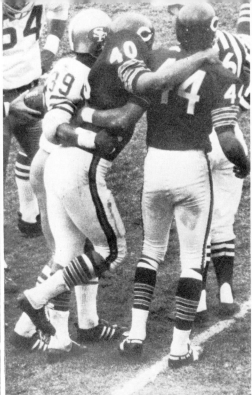

Alexander (39) and teammate Garry Lyle (44) help Gale off the field after his injury.

In May 1968, George Halas finally stepped down as head coach. Jim Dooley took over. The season was full of ups and downs for the team. The Bears were four and four in late November, when they faced the San Francisco 49ers. Gale had rushed 856 yards and seemed to be heading for his best season ever.

Then, when Gale was trying to cut around the 49er defense on an ordinary play, disaster struck. Gale's cleats were anchored in the turf. Kermit Alexander of the 49ers hit him with a low block. The force bent Gale's right knee completely sideways.

He went down, then tried to get up. Alexander looked at him anxiously. "It's gone," Gale said. "The knee is gone."

Brian Piccolo makes a gain against the Washington Redskins.

Brian Piccolo went in as halfback and the Bears won the game. Gale went to the hospital and had a long operation to repair his torn-up knee. It was the kind of injury that had ruined many a football career. Even though the doctor repaired the damage, Gale faced a long recovery. He had to do painful exercises to make the knee work again. And always there were doubts: even if the knee worked, would he be able to run as well as before?

After successful surgery to repair his knee, Gale faced many months of painful exercise to put the leg back into shape.

Leaning against a goalpost, Gale watches the Bears work out.

He had endless workouts at the Y, building himself up again. His friends tried to cheer him up when he doubted that he would make it. One newspaperman wrote: "Even if Sayers makes a comeback, he may be finished as a runner. He may have to consider playing another position."

That made Gale mad. He cut out the article. "I'm going to come back. And when I do, that writer is going to have to eat this piece of paper!"

He came to training camp in the summer of 1969 feeling good. The Hall of Fame had picked him, along with Jim Brown, for the All-Time Pro Football Team first string. It was a great honor, reflecting his past glory—but Gale was more interested in the future.

He played with pain. But he refused to pamper himself in practice and seemed to be as fast as ever.

Then came the first exhibition game, on a rainy night in Washington, D.C. The Redskin kickoff came straight to Gale.

He started up the middle, then began faking and swerving as well as he ever had. In the end zone after a 94-yard run, he knew he had made it. Later the officials said he had run out of bounds—but it didn't matter.

Next morning, Gale read in the papers: "It took the sellout crowd only a matter of seconds to see for themselves that Gale Sayers is as good as ever."

Gale makes a gain during a game against the St. Louis Cardinals.

Of course it wasn't that easy. The knee hurt and it also tired easily. Gale kept on pushing himself and did a heroic job of rushing. It looked like he was heading for another rushing title.

But the Bears won only a single game.

Brian Piccolo still backed Gale up. And his close friendship, more than that of any other teammate, helped give Gale confidence again.

In this game against the Rams, Gale scored a TD and carried 15 times for 109 yards. But Los Angeles won, 9-7.

Brian Piccolo backed Gale up in many 1969 games. Here Brian is stopped by Jack Pardee of the Rams *(32)*. Despite several operations, Brian Piccolo died of cancer on June 16, 1970. He was 26 years old.

In November, Brian Piccolo had to go for a chest x-ray because of a bad cough. The doctors found a spot on his lung. "You can't play in the Baltimore game next Sunday," they told him.

Gale found out about Brian's illness on Friday. Tests had revealed chest cancer in the 26-year-old halfback. Gale visited his friend and they joked about it. Then Brian went to a New York hospital for an operation while Gale stood up in front of the team and said:

"You know Brian Piccolo is very sick. I think we should all give our best effort to win this ball game and give the game ball to Pic. . . ."

They played their hearts out against the Baltimore Colts. And with six minutes to go, they were ahead, 21-14. But then the Colts intercepted a pass and scored. In the remaining minutes of play, they managed a field goal. The Bears had tried to "win one for Pic," but the 1969 jinx had them licked.

Brian Piccolo's cancer operation seemed to be a success. He joked a lot with Gale about the poor showing the team made, finishing the season 1-13-0.

However, Gale was league rushing champion again with 1,032 yards. He also carried the ball more than anyone else—236 attempts. It was one of football's outstanding comebacks.

Howard Mudd *(68)* runs interference for Gale in a 1969 game.

Bill Guthrie, President of the Pro Football Writers of America, presents Gale Sayers with the Most Courageous Player Award.

Brian Piccolo grew worse. Gale had the same type of blood as his friend and donated a pint. Later, Brian said: "I feel fine, but lately I have this awful craving for chitlins!"

Gale laughed, but his heart was full of sorrow. Doctors had told him that Brian Piccolo was dying.

In May 1970 the Professional Football Writers Association had their annual banquet. They gave Gale Sayers the George S. Halas Award as the most courageous player in the sport.

Gale told them: "You flatter me by giving me this award. But I accept it for Brian Piccolo. It's mine tonight, but it'll be his tomorrow."

They were extraordinary words. But Gale Sayers had never wanted to be an ordinary man.

GALE EUGENE SAYERS

He was born May 30, 1943 in Wichita, Kansas, the second son of Roger Winfield Sayers and Bernice Ross Sayers. His father's people had been pioneer Kansas settlers; his great-uncle, W. L. Sayers, was the first black county attorney in Kansas.

Gale graduated from Omaha Central High School in 1961. He attended the University of Kansas for four years, but lacking 10 hours of credits, did not graduate. He and his wife, the former Linda McNeil, have three children.

Gale's other leg was injured in an exhibition game in 1970. In the regular season, he carried the ball only 23 times for 52 yards before he was sidelined for another operation. His legs were never the same after that. Even though he worked hard to strengthen them, he was able to rush only 13 times for 38 yards in 1971. On September 10, 1972, he announced that he would retire.

In addition to working as a stockbroker, Gale spends time with youth groups and writes a newspaper column. In 1970 he wrote his autobiography, *I Am Third.* It refers to his motto: "The Lord is first, my friends are second, and I am third." The story of his remarkable friendship with Brian Piccolo became a television drama, *Brian's Song,* that was seen by more than 48 million people.

In 1973, Gale Sayers joined the coaching staff of the University of Kansas.

RECORDS

Most points, rookie season: 132 in 1965
Most touchdowns, season: 22 in 1965
Most touchdowns, rookie season: 22 in 1965
Most touchdowns, game: 6 (tied with Ernie Nevers and Dub Jones)
Most touchdowns, kickoff returns, lifetime: 6 (tied with Ollie Matson)
Most yards gained, season: 2440 in 1966
Highest average gain, game: 19.76 on Dec. 12, 1965
Highest kickoff return average: 30.56

NFL scoring champ: 1965 with 22 touchdowns
NFL rushing champ
1966: 1231 yds.
1969: 1032 yds.

Rookie of the Year: 1965

All-League Selection: 1965, 1966, 1967, 1968, 1969

George S. Halas Award: 1970